Cling to the Magic

Mere Mortals

by

Daveda Gruber

©2009 Daveda Gruber
All rights reserved. No part of this book may be reproduced, stored in retrieval system or transmitted in any form by any means without the prior permission of the publishers. With the exception of a reviewer who may quote brief passages in a review to be printed in a newspaper, magazine or journal.
ISBN: 978-1-4092-9015-5

This book

is

Dedicated

to

Joree Williams

and

Helen McManus

Thank you Ladies,

Yes, I Can!

Acknowledgements

**Cover and Heading Graphic Artwork
by
Daveda Gruber**

**Introduction and Back Cover
by
Daveda Gruber**

**Editing
by
Daveda Gruber**

**All Interior and Exterior Formatting
by
Daveda Gruber**

Introduction

Daveda Gruber is an extremely versatile and well known writer of this era. Gruber has fourteen books published but felt the need to revise this; her eight book. It is now truly a magical read. Gruber clings to the magic in her life and creates magic for others.

Daveda has an imagination that can make you laugh or cry. She writes books for adults and beautiful children's books. Gruber writes novels and poetry.

Over the years, Daveda has studied many poetic styles/forms. She loves a challenge, as you will see in this book, the more difficult the poetic style, the more it strengthens her determination to be the best that she can be.

After being on many Internet sites, Gruber decided it was time to start her own poetry site. Fortitude on her part had already made her a publisher and now she owns her own publishing company and works closely with a team. If you knew her, you would expect this.

Daveda has now graciously decided to help others learn to write poetic forms. In this book you will find over forty poetic styles used in an array of ways to delight and enchant you.

If you just want to read some excellent poetic verse, pick up this book and buy it. You will never regret your

decision. The pages will entertain and absorb your interest and have you wanting to explore the writings of Daveda Gruber.

Table of Contents

Cling to the Magic..1
Sweet Dreams..3
Where Angels Dance..5
Majesty to Behold..7
Magical Place..9
Night Kiss.. 11
Obsession to Beguile.....................................13
Gifts of Love 15
My Civics Test..17
My Birthday Gift...19
An American!...21
I Am an American..23
Metal Tiger..25
Daveda Gruber...27
Princess Star...29
Sonny 31
A Walk with the Sun......................................32
Bittersweet Wine...38
Butterfly..40
Witch Holiday..41
Masks That Fright...43
Trick or Treat...45
Pot of Gold..46
Leprechauns...48

Mirrored Souls..50
I Know Helen McManus!...............................52
I Know Joree!...54
A Good Start..56
Fun in the Sun... 57
Gracing Paradise...58
The Wedding...60
Never Far Away.. 62
Abandon to Soar...66
Dreams Glimmering Love.............................68
Sister...70
Curls..72
Loving..73
Precious Moments..74
Orange Flowers...76
With Love to Give... 78
Passion Unsurpassed...................................80
Ice Storm...83
In Force...85
Fairy Dust..87
Not Alone..89
Rushing Waves...91
Tranquil Waters..92
Gift to Tempt You...94
Discovering...97
Love..99

Magic Fairies..100
No Title..102
Overcome..103
Dreams Unfolding......................................104
Integrity of Your Way................................106
My Essence Sings......................................108
Teardrop...110
Gazing at Stars...112
Autumn Has Begun....................................114
Blonde of All Trades..................................116
Don't See What to Wear............................119
She Dances on Air....................................121
Magical Dust...123
World Peace..125
World in Her Hand....................................127
Within Salvation..129
Mere Mortals...131
Glossary..133-146

Cling to the Magic
(Rhyming Couplets)

**A world and beyond within our reach;
magnificently displayed to each.**

**Cling to the magic before it fades;
for in its place behold the charades.**

Desires fulfilled vanishing promptly;
shortly to be a fait accompli.

Dreams of hope held as reality;
now, tossed aside with formality.

Let not my imagination melt;
where last remaining emotions felt.

~*~

Sweet Dreams
(Pantoum)

Wishing life was lived in sweet dreams;
purple clouds and azure blue sky.
Glitter floats from flowers, it seems;
swirls of rose and pinks flying high.

Purple clouds and azure blue sky;
birds are singing and fairies play.
Swirls of rose and pinks flying high;
everyone has nice words to say.

Birds are singing and fairies play;
sun smiles; lush emerald grass grows.
Everyone has nice words to say.
Light gentle breeze tickles and blows.

Sun smiles; lush emerald grass grows;
glitter floats from flowers, it seems.
Light gentle breeze tickles and blows;
wishing life was lived in sweet dreams.

~*~

Where Angels Dance
(Daveda's Angel)

Where
do angels
dance?
Sanction my aptitude: grace me in trance.
My wishes to float among stars,
where never foe does travel;
able to release scars.
Sorrows unravel;
grant me
delight.
Space without fright;
unrestrained up high
deeming love is power.
Silence music of the sky,
angels dance as they empower.
Pure entity engrossed with beauty;
defining ultimate sense to feel free.

~*~

Majesty to Behold
(Rhyming Couplets)

Bursting with mystical knowledge within;
hidden inside a sad heart, mortal sin.

Golden locks framed majesty to behold.
Said by many, her future was foretold.

They called her a goddess, Freya by name.
No earthly man did know from where she came.

Voice laced with silk brought men to Freya's feet.
One gaze in azure eyes; naught could retreat.

Searching earth and sky, for her true love, Od;
banished to the sea, although a great God.

Freya's passion was frocking with men.
Even though married, she had over ten.

For her husband's never ending pursuit,
instincts led her to sea, she was astute.

Hideous sea monster, Od had become;
now to stay by his side she had succumb.

When slaughtered as the creature he became,
congenial visits they could now both claim.

~*~

Freya: Norse Goddess of love, beauty and sensuality also of war and death.

Magical Place
(Rubiyat)

When darkness covers and eyes close,
soothing wind with gentleness blows.
Appearing, as a scenic dream,
a magical place where love glows.

An enchanting princess so grand,
with winged aide who flies to her hand,
sits atop a wide open throne.
With a pure heart, she rules the land.

Stars dance and fairies play all night.
Princess sings as she twinkles bright.
As the sun rises, magic sleeps;
waiting in rest for more delight.

~*~

Night Kiss
(Rhyming Couplets)

**Night breeze caresses my cheek like a kiss;
lets many thoughts wonder and reminisce.**

**Gazing up, a twinkle shines from my eye;
seeing the flutter of wings up so high.**

**Precious child, the heavens sparkle for you;
to very edges of the sky you flew.**

**My special angel you will always be;
until I meet you for eternity.**

~*~

Author's Note:
In memory of my first daughter Lanie,
November 18, 1968-January 9, 2004.

Obsession to Beguile
(Metered Quatrain)

Irresistible are her luscious charms;
invitation of much desired passion.
Craving to be in stately beauty's arms;
fortunate, to be dealt your small ration.

**Exquisite goddess far above the rest;
Aphrodite will consume your control.
Her ally Cupid renders you obsessed;
lustful yearning possessing entire soul.**

**She will titillate you with just one smile;
sensation which exceeds expectation.
Goddess with an obsession to beguile;
mortal man cannot escape temptation.**

~*~

Aphrodite:
daughter of Zeus, King of the Gods, and Dione, an early earth/mother goddess gorgeous, perfect, eternally young woman, potent sexual attractiveness, dazzling beauty.

10 Syllable Quatrain with rhyme scheme of:
a,b,a,b,c,d,c,d,e,f,e,f

Gifts of Love

(Rhyming Couplets)

When much seems lost and dreary,
existing becomes weary.

Reaching to glimpse at beauty;
feeling your love on duty.

Giving thanks to Him above,
for I receive gifts of love.

Even though I'm still not well;
with true love, my heart does swell.

Sonny you've been more than kind;
finer husband; could not find!

This poem is one day late;
we'll wait for that "special date!"

~*~

My Civics Test
(Free Style)

Studying really hard to ace this test;
for a woman my age, I'll do my best.
A permanent resident is not enough.
I must be the best that I can be
because I live in the land of the free.

I have a website where poets depend
on reviews from me; I feel like a friend.
Hope that you can all bear though this;
knowing with the will inside my heart
that all poets are pretty smart.

When this test of my knowledge is past,
I'll feel a part of this country, at last.
Now, I cannot vote or state my case.
One hundred questions I can show
to all of you who want to know.

Please understand my limitations,
now with time devoted to this nation.
Wishing to become a citizen
of this country where I rest my head;
got to be a reason why here, I was led.

~*~

My Birthday Gift
(Metered Quatrain)

This birthday will be special indeed,
be off to Pittsburgh the night before.
In the early morning to proceed
to Federal building on eighth floor.

Best birthday present could ever get;
to be sworn in to this great country.
November twentieth, can't forget;
American in land of the free.

Just got this news, and wanted to share
with all the great poets, on my site.
For in my heart, I know my friends care.
You're friendship is clear, of that I'm right.

If you have a bash, I won't be here.
You'll be in my thoughts, I guarantee!
Sonny says we'll party; have no fear.
My Birthday; American I'll be!

~*~

I am to be sworn in as an AMERICAN on my birthday, November 20th. Now, that is a GREAT BIRTHDAY GIFT!

Quatrain format: a,b,a,b,c,d,c,d,e,f,e,f,g,h,g,h rhyme scheme, 9 syllables per line.

An American!
(Rhyming Couplets)

Pittsburgh had a party for me;
citizen in 'Land of the Free.'

My Birthday celebration grand;
as I took my oath in this land.

U.S. knows how to throw a bash
Turned out to be quite a splash!

My Sonny took me out to eat;
the place he picked could not be beat!

Look at the Menu, all for me.
All food looked nice; you must agree!

THE STEAKHOUSE

Happy Birthday, Daveda!
November 20, 2009

APPETIZERS

Tuna Tartare *Diced Tomato and Avocado, Thai Cream and Balsamic Glaze**	15
Smoked Pacific Salmon	14
Maine Lobster Cocktail *Mustard Mayonnaise & Cocktail Sauces*	20
Jumbo Lump Crabmeat Cocktail *Mustard Mayonnaise Sauce*	15
Broiled Sea Scallops Wrapped in Bacon *Apricot Chutney*	16
Colossal Shrimp Cocktail	20
Oysters on the Half Shell*	15
Oysters Rockefeller, *Classic Preparation**	15
Jumbo Lump Crab Cake, *Mustard Mayonnaise Sauce*	14
Colossal Shrimp Alexander, *Beurre Blanc Sauce*	18
Baked Five Onion Soup, *Crusted with Swiss Cheese*	10
Lobster Bisque	14

MORTON'S PRIME OCEAN PLATTERS

CHILLED serves two 43 serves three to four 86 serves five to six 128⁵⁰
Maine Lobster, Colossal Shrimp Cocktail, Jumbo Lump Crabmeat, Oysters on the Half Shell*, Alaskan King Crab Legs

BAKED serves two 42 serves three to four 84 serves five to six 126
Sea Scallops Wrapped in Bacon, Jumbo Lump Crab Cakes, Oysters Rockefeller, Colossal Shrimp Alexander

SALADS

Center Cut Iceberg	11
Our Version of the Wedge, with Chopped Egg, Tomato, Bacon Bits and either Morton's Blue Cheese Dressing or Thousand Island Dressing	
Caesar Salad, *Classic Dressing*	10
Morton's Salad *Morton's Blue Cheese Dressing, Chopped Egg, Anchovies*	10
Sliced Beefsteak Tomato *Purple Onion and Vinaigrette or Morton's Blue Cheese*	10⁵⁰
Chopped Salad	11
Iceberg & Romaine Lettuce, Hearts of Palm, Artichoke Hearts, Bacon, Blue Cheese, Chopped Egg, Purple Onion, Tomato, and Avocado with a Dijon Mustard Vinaigrette	

SIDE DISHES

Steamed Fresh Jumbo Asparagus *Hollandaise Sauce*	10⁰⁰
Grilled Jumbo Asparagus *Balsamic Glaze*	10⁵⁰
Sauteed Garlic Green Beans	7⁵⁰
Steamed Fresh Broccoli *Hollandaise Sauce*	9

Creamed Spinach, *for Two*	10⁵⁰
Sauteed Fresh Spinach & Button Mushrooms	8
Sauteed Button Mushrooms	9
Jumbo Baked Idaho® Potato	8⁵⁰
Hashbrown Potato, *for Two*	9⁵⁰
Lyonnaise Potatoes	8⁵⁰
Mashed Potatoes	9
Potato Skins	8
French Fries	8
Macaroni & Cheese, *Hint of Spice*	10⁵⁰

ENTREES

Double Cut Filet Mignon, *Bearnaise Sauce**	43
Porterhouse Steak*	49
Double Porterhouse, *for Two, Carved Tableside**	98
New York Strip Steak, *Signature Cut**	49
Chicago Style Bone-In Ribeye Steak*	49
Prime Rib	49
Bone-In Double Cut ... Available Friday & Saturday only*	

MORTON'S *"slightly smaller"* STEAKS

New York Strip Steak*	43
Single Cut Filet Mignon *Bearnaise Sauce**	38
Filet Oskar *Asparagus, Jumbo Lump Crab, Bearnaise Sauce**	43
Ribeye Steak*	40
Cajun Ribeye Steak*	42

Au Poivre, Five Peppercorn Cognac Cream Sauce added to any steak...five dollars

Domestic Double Rib Lamb Chops*	41
Chicken Christopher, *Garlic Beurre Blanc Sauce*	27
Sesame Encrusted Yellowfin Tuna *Spicy Soy Ginger Sauce**	35
Broiled Salmon Fillet, *Chef's Beurre Blanc Sauce**	31
Jumbo Lump Crab Cakes *Mustard Mayonnaise Sauce*	40
Colossal Shrimp Alexander, *Beurre Blanc Sauce*	37

Alaskan King Crab Legs	58
or as an accompaniment to any steak	29
Lobster Tail, *Western Australian*	42
Jumbo Lobster Tail, *Western Australian*	55
Whole Baked Maine Lobster	market price

*Consuming raw or undercooked meats, poultry, seafood or shellfish may increase your risk of foodborne illness, especially if you have certain medical conditions.

T2/0609

Only thing missing that transcends;
not being with my poet friends!

~*~

I Am an American
(Rhyming Couplets)

Choosing to reside in this land
when a wedding for me was planned.

Came here to the land of the free;
legally the way it should be.

Permanent resident; I became.
Was proud of status; did acclaim.

Love for this country and her flag
had need to do something to brag.

An American was my goal.
This great county was in my soul.

Studied for my citizen's test;
calculated to do my best.

Passed with flying colors, test met,
am an American; you bet!

~*~

Metal Tiger
(Rhyming Couplets)

My fierce sign in Chinese astrology;
the tiger who gives no apology.

I believe what I speak, in my own mind;
quick witted and charming, I can be kind.

A fine hostess, entertaining with love;
a know it all, ego is to boast of.

Hardworking but liking some time to play;
always wanting things to go my own way.

Love to run free with the rules only mine.
Impulsive, don't know where to draw the line.

Unstructured need, can lead to regret this;
daring to take many risks, finding bliss.

I've been known to jump right in with two feet;
pretension and injustice stand and meet.

Go to extremes, intense and possessive.
Watch out, this tiger can be aggressive!

Element of this tiger is metal.
Earth, wood, fire, or water; won't settle.

Sometimes mask is put on to hide feelings.
Remember that if we have some dealings.

Gay abandon, dancing to my own tune,
right on my own stage so that all may swoon.

From unattainable untried why hide?
Myriad of colors; my carrousel ride!

~*~

DAVEDA GRUBER

(Acrostic-Rhymed)

Destined to write from a young age;
A woman who knows when to turn the page.
Vivacious and ready to help friends;
Everyone knows the love she extends.
Demanding loyalty is one of her traits.
Asking for fairness it what she states.

Grateful for integrity that comes her way;
Ready to listen to what others say.
Undamaged by obstacles in her life;
Believing she tries to be a good wife.
Ecstatic with the smallest of things;
Realizes what goodness brings.

~*~

Princess Star
(Rhyming Couplets)

Princess Star lived in up high;
home far away past clouds in the sky.

Free spirit on a throne of gold stars;
ruling through the darkness until dawn.

Her beauty was known throughout the night;
glow form Star maiden made the land bright.

Unicorn of violet came to hear
of this pure maiden who did appear.

Star on his horn guided him to her.
As myth has it, interest it did spur.

When a purple lit sky can be seen,
unicorn is carrying his queen.

~*~

Sonny
(Clerihew)

In cyberspace, I stumbled on Sonny.
When we met, could tell he was a honey.
Wrote love poems about this handsome man.
It seems that now, he has many a fan!

~*~

A Walk with the Sun
(Rhyming Couplets)

It was very early in the morning.
All was quiet, except I heard birds sing.

Fragrant air with a mélange of flowers;
opened wide from refreshing rain showers.

What a beautiful day to take a walk;
I started on my way at eight o'clock.

**In the forest, I was compelled to go.
When my eyes looked up, someone said, "Hello."**

**Then the smiling sun asked, "How do you do?"
"Just fine," I replied, "Can I walk with you?"**

**"Sure," smiled the sun, "I'll be up here all day!"
"Have a nice time while I brighten your way!"**

**My greatest adventure had now begun.
"What is your name please?" I asked of the sun.**

**"Sonny is my name, tell me, who are you?"
"I'm Daveda; I'm enjoying the view"**

Turning my head, bumped into two strange guys;
no fear on this trip, turned out to be wise.

They told me my walk would be very long;
said, "Don't stop because nothing will go wrong."

This adventure was fun as I sat down;
where we were we going, would there be a town?

Feeling tired; I needed a little rest.
Butterflies sat close by; this was the best!

It started to get dark, I met more friends;
night creatures that live on after life ends.

Still, I was not daunted by what I saw;
I knew this journey would have not a flaw!

**Now it was late and Sonny said, "Goodnight!"
What would happen to me without bright light?**

"Fear not sweet Daveda, I have a plan."
All of a sudden, Sonny the sun ran!

I blinked and saw soft lighting around me.
I was up in the sky floating so free!

**Where was the sun; I sure did miss his hue.
Suddenly, the moon was there in clear view!**

**We became lovers that night in the sky;
under the stars; love begins and that's why!**

Bittersweet Wine
(Quatrain Metered)

Holding what, when freedom is not mine?
Decisions lie not within my reach.
Tasting once again bittersweet wine;
even as words implore and beseech.

**Knowledge held makes not one empowered;
acknowledged deception meant to fool.
Elation turned and becomes soured;
breaking free from restraints and will rule.**

**Bubble of glass shatters to release
supremacy to take hold of reign.
Instance smoothly begins to increase;
comprehension known way to attain.**

~*~

BUTTERFLY
(Wordsmith)

Breeze brushes by
Unusually unique; unruffled.
Tenderly touches trippingly
Tasting tempting thirst-quencher.
Endlessly excelling excellence;
Representing radiance rising.
Finding flickering flight;
Loveliness lays luminous
Yielding yet yearned.

~*~

Witch Holiday
(Rhyming Couplets)

Spooky is this night.
Fear with all your might!

Watch where you're waking,
do not be talking.

Many witches out;
making people shout.

Turn your head up high;
ghosts fly in the sky.

Witches making brew,
a ghoulish hot stew.

Children screaming loud;
on this night allowed.

Look up to the moon.
Witch will be here soon!

A witch holiday;
one will fly your way.

Cackling will be heard.
Scary is her word.

Avoid any witch;
don't fall for her pitch!

Halloween will pass.
She'll run out of gas!

Love getting candy.
This is so dandy!

~*~

MASKS THAT FRIGHT

(Abecedarian)

Arranging the house,
Because it's time to douse;
Covering outside the door,
Drenched in gore.
Eerie things around;
Freaky creatures on the ground.
Getting rather scary here;
Horror closer; all should fear.
I still love this night;
Jack 'O Lanterns shinning bright.
Keeping the path lit;
Light the way, don't quit!
Maybe you can find a treat,
No one can say you're beat!
Open your eyes;
Prepare for cries.
Quiet now and listen,
Running feet now glisten.
Snow is floating in the air!
Telling to be careful what we wear!
Under the gloomy sky,
Visions of what makes us cry!
Wearing masks that fright;
X-ray vision would help your plight.
Yes, this is Halloween my friend
Zestfully, my invitation I extend!

~*~

Trick or Treat
(Lanturne String)

Come
get scared
ghosts flying
witches brewing
fear

You
beware
dread goblins
All Hallows Eve
near

Want
candy
Trick or Treat
will you get some
ask

Carved
pumpkins
to spook you
it's Halloween
BOO
~*~

Pot of Gold
(Rhyming Couplets)

**Fables whispered faintly at times;
focus on echoes of wind chimes.**

**Hidden within subtle refrain
through melodies, riddles obtain.**

**Alluring charm exposed in green;
enticed by her spirit serene.**

**Pot of gold not swindled with ease;
splendor clad in green will appease.**

**Attaining treasured gold, concealed;
inside puzzle, promptly revealed.**

Leprechauns
(Rhyming Couplets)

Although bright color green,
Leprechauns are unseen.

Hiding not to be caught,
for what they have is sought.

It is said he has gold;
his riches are untold.

Catch him and gain his wealth.
Keep your eyes in good health.

If you lose sight of him,
he'll be off in a whim!

~*~

Mirrored Souls
(Daveda's Quatre-Rime-Par-Huit)

Covering your back with might;
tougher to lose sight.
Two as one
try.
Mirrored souls guided by light,
jointly aiding plight,
together
win.

Iniquity is curtailed.
Malicious unveiled;
as triumph
heard.
Watching sinful acts detailed.
Honesty prevailed;
unruffled
won.

~*~

Author's Note:
This poem is dedicated to my friend Carol A. Eckart.

I Know Helen McManus!
(Joree's 2 Line Finish)

Ally you can't replace;
lady full of such grace.
a heart filled full with her friends;
caring words Helen extends
when needed.

~*~

A laugh to bring us joy;
no doubt you will enjoy.
Always ready for some fun.
From a joke she'll never run;
she will stay.

~*~

An animal lover;
easy to discover.
Family important in life;
quiet when she deals with strife
her own way.

~*~

Author's Note:
This was a Challenge by Joree Williams.

I Know Joree!
(Abecedarian)
*I Know Someone ...Joree Williams Challenge

A woman who is remarkable!
Better than most at what she does;
Caring of all people.
Doing things to help others;
Everyone loves her.
Friends all know she is
Gentle and sweet as can be.
Has books published but has an
Insatiable need to improve.
Joree is her name and she is so
Kind in everything she does.
Loving lady with a big heart, you
Must get to know her.
Never has a bad word to say;
Oh what a delight to identify with her!
Pleasure to have as a friend;
Quietly she does so much for others.
Ready to lend a hand when needed;
Satisfaction is hers by helping.
Truly a hard working lady;
Usually works too relentlessly!
Vivacious even when not feeling well;
Williams is her last name.
Xanadu claims her as its first citizen; she
Yields an imagination so very rare.
Zealous in every way; we love Joree!
~*~

A Good Start
(Cywydd devair fyrion)

Open your heart.
It's a good start.

Love who you are;
you will get far.

Let kindness flow;
your love will show.

Soon you will see,
love returns free!

~*~

Fun in the Sun
(Septolet)

Fun
away
in the sun.
Play every day!

Feel so free
with glee;
me!

~*~

Gracing Paradise
(Rhyming Couplets)

**Precious angels although distant;
your protection is consistent.**

**Beyond clouds and azure blue skies,
sensations of which I surmise.**

**Frolicking amongst moonbeam lights;
together engaging in flights.**

**Cherished loved ones singing for me;
whereas in heaven, floating free.**

**Gracing paradise lovingly;
bestowing comfort caringly.**

**Sheltering my own existence;
showering love with persistence.**

~*~

Author's Note:
This poem was written in memory of my daughter Lanie and my sister Sharon. ('Shari the Lion-Hearted')

The Wedding
(Rhyming Coupets)

It happened a very long time ago;
story about beautiful love did grow.

Family on both sides forever kind;
some of the nicest people you could find.

Most are in heaven but some of them here;
all of them held close in my heart so dear.

Macky and Sonia brought to life three girls;
one with straight hair and two with pretty curls.

Gave Mom and Dad three grandchildren to love;
Dad met one, two came when he was above.

Looking back I see a family fine;
proud to say I still consider them mine.

~*~

NEVER FAR AWAY

(Shakesspearean Sonnet)

He would forever be her baby boy;
two girls, then the son she longed for was born.
He bestowed on his dear mother such joy.
All of her love, on him, she would adorn.
The boy slowly turns into a grown man.
A strong bond has been created for life.
He visits her every day when he can,
even though he has children and a wife.
He can do no wrong in her loving eyes.
Kisses on her forehead, he always gives.
Her last day on earth, he holds her and cries;
thinking of his mother each day he lives.

He visits her grave until his last day;
buried beside her, never far away.

~*~

Abandon to Soar
(Metered Quatrain)

Cage not an angel who desires flight;
she may hold yearning to reach new height.
Dreams held within her soul; let ignite.
Be it day, or path into late night.

Freedom gives chance to open her wings.
By means of liberty her heart sings.
For deep within her contentment rings;
yielding to all elation she brings.
To be unaided; she will not plead.
Requirements she has of her need.
Independence assists to proceed;
alone she must take flight to succeed.

Give forth not a callous mighty roar;
let her not have the need to implore.
By her side grant candor to explore;
she gives the dove abandon to soar.

~*~

Author's Note:
Mono-Rhymed Stanzas

Her Castle
(Rubiyat)

In a castle way north of here,
ventures a princess without fear.
Relishing on icy water;
through the fog, her voice you can hear.

Singing a sad tune to the wind
of dreams lost and left far behind.
Chill in her blood obstructs cold breeze;
condemned victim of deeds maligned.

No name she carries which is known;
doom being surviving alone.
With the elements she subsists.
Never love to her shall be shown.

Long ago having forgiven
the ill-fate her life was given.
As morning sun gives light and warms,
in her castle she is driven.

~*~

Author's Note:
Picture Challenge by Terry E. Eckart.

Dreams Glimmering Love
(Quatrain)

Stars twinkle so brightly all around
gazing to the heavens for answers.
Dark of night brings calmness without sound;
yet sky is much consumed with dancers.

In quiet of bright stars up above,
my mind travels to hope gone with fate.
In weathered hands dreams glimmering love;
t'is gone the times past to sit and wait.

Future gives glitter; craft false wishes.
Time has laid down wicked time on earth.
Eyes close as the light beams yields swishes;
nighttime sky gives this sadness worth.

Time takes light traveling to my soul;
embodies outer being gently.
Life wanted, taken away, just stole.
Searching stars; dreams life differently.

~*~

Author's Note:
Picture Challenge by Terry E. Eckart.

SISTER

(Acrostic-Rhymed)

Memories forever are shared by two;
Yesterday's dreams not always came true.

Streams of tears blending as one;
Intermingling, if we lost or won.
Sharing moments good and bad;
Together facing times happy and sad.
Enduring deaths as they came to pass;
Reminded of difficulties we had to surpass.

Gloria, the time came to go our own ways.
Love still pulled through those days.
Our hearts have a place, as sisters do;
Ribbons and bows hold love so true.
I wrapped up a tiny box in my heart;
A gift for you that cannot come apart.

Aurthor's Note:
My sister, Gloria, has had her share of illness this past year.
She was given seven more years to live a while back.

Curls
(THAN-BAUK)

My hair looks nice.
A fair price paid.
Entice with curls!

~*~

Loving
(Ameri-ku)

**Loving Sonny so much;
oh yes, we love to touch.
Staying by his side;
makes me warm inside.
Never get cold;
have him to hold!**

~*~

Precious Moments
(Ottava Rima)

Dreams fulfilled as stimulation appears.
Darkness illuminated aligned with night.
Floating upwards buoyantly; without fears;
as heaven takes on overwhelming sight.

**Daytime disillusionment disappears,
as essence of soul, elevates through height.
Relishing in escapade; pleased to climb
those ecstatic precious moments in time.**

~*~

Orange Flowers
(Limerick)

In Niagara Falls went out to eat.
Sitting by the water was so neat!

A nice lunch near the 'Falls.'
Close to hear 'water calls!'

A pretty flower just looked so sweet!

~*~

Orange flowers put on each table.
Told to eat mine; must be a fable!

Saw tables they were on;
noticed many were gone.

Couldn't eat a flower with no label!

~*~

Sonny and I find good spots to go;
fine restaurant with the 'Falls' below.

Could not eat a flower;
had not the will-power!

Adventure sure cost Sonny much 'dough!'

~*~

With Love to Give
(Renga)

My husband is kind;
lovingly he holds me tight.
The best I could find.

~~*~~

Went to Canada to meet;
a woman I met was sweet.

~~*~~

Not from here, I'm told.
Was born far in a land north;
left because I'm bold.

~~*~~

Found a love with golden hair;
such a beauty that stands fair.

~~*~~

Born with skin so white,
brown eyed blond with love to give,
a woman who wants to write.

~~*~~

Squeezing her with all my might;
makes my whole day feel so bright.

~~*~~

Quickly fell in love;
he makes the world spin for me;
marriage from above.

~*~

Passion Unsurpassed
(Ballade)

Stars twinkle awaiting a glow.
Moon gleams at two lovers at night.
Inner knowledge where they will go;
through their eyes a picturesque sight.
Warmth as they hold each other tight;
releasing what has been the past.
Together ambiance feels right.
Passion will never be surpassed.

Whispers of love in the wind blow.
Togetherness just feels alright.
Gift for each other will bestow
essence of sensing delight.
Flames within will always ignite;
fire inside lovers has been cast.
Two as one forever shine bright.
Passion will never be surpassed.

Fervor to each other will grow;
paths to pleasure tend to excite.
Reaching beyond stars; new plateau
far beyond any dreamed of height.
Soaring to the moon; love takes flight.
Pace built up; emotions run fast.
No looking back; let come what might.
Passion will never be surpassed.

Adoration we will incite.
Desire justly spills unsurpassed,
access open, we will invite.
Passion will never be surpassed.

~*~

Ice Storm
(Katauta Suite)

**Crystal flakes descend
Grassland blades frozen rigid
Tree branches exposed to ice**

**Hail strikes with great force
Frost crushing fragile nature
Encompassing land**

**Icy is cold ground
Sheet of sheer glass dangerous
Animals slipping**

~*~

In Force
(Tanka Suite)

Ice scorches the earth
Winter has damaged pure soil
Seasons keep cycle

Chilling wind bites at small buds
Bitter frost clawing to stay

∼∼*∼∼

Frost has won for now
Wintry iciness still clings
Hope for change still waits

Morning sun brings warmth
Gentle breeze tenderly smiles

~~*~~

Beauty uplifting
Beckons enticing flowers
Tiny bird feels safe

Danger lurks fulfils hunger
Nature's cycle still in force

~*~

Fairy Dust
(Shadow Sonnet)

Must meet fairies loving them is a must.
Sing a song with them of beauty they sing.
Dust is lucky they sprinkle fairy dust.
Bring an open mind for fortune they bring.

Truth is their tale for fairies bring you truth.
Cry not; for fairies bring no tears to cry.
Youth will encompass they own gift of youth.
Fly nearby delicate winged creature fly.

**Night you will see them they fly in the night
Charming and tiny you'll feel them charming.
Sight must be keen if you get one in sight.
Harming no one, you'll nay see one harming.**

**Enchanted creature deems you enchanted.
Granted is a wish from fairy granted.**

~*~

Not Alone
(Rhyming Couplets)

They were in love from the day they met.
Her face was one he could not forget.

In hopes one day he would hear her call;
has looked at her picture on the wall.

Carefully stepping, making his way;
focusing on his mission this day.

Feeble feet move slowly to the row;
without looking, he knows where to go.

Her stone beckoned to him every time;
the way she was murdered was a crime.

She was loved by two handsome young men;
one was named James the other one Ben.

With the shot from a gun, she had died;
as Ben took his own life, James had cried.

He could never marry in his life;
his love was for his first choice of wife.

The cemetery was where he felt peace;
true love was not one ever to cease.

He saw her face in front of his own;
a voice said, "Come, you are not alone."

She took his hand, together they rose,
hand in hand they went; where the wind blows.

~*~

Rushing Waves
(Nonet)

Follow my teardrops and take my hand
Walk along my side in the sand
Hear the roar of rushing waves
As they hit the beach caves
My feet will guide us
Naught to discuss
To the sea
With me
Flee

~*~

Tranquil Waters
(Quatrain)

Wheel revolves as cool water flows;
spinning in circles now as time.
Just as beginning of life grows
from a babe then into our prime.

Moments through lives water runs still.
As wheel of life, water gets rough.
Gushes of our entity spill;
turbulence can make living rough.

As water moves, so do the years.
Constant stream transports with it age.
Tranquil waters take away tears.
Hope helps to gently turn the page.

Cooling our souls like a fresh stream;
dampening the rage stretched past.
Aged wood, like our being, has gleam.
While here, permit beauty to last.

~*~

Author's Note:
A Challenge by Carol A. Eckart

Gift to Tempt You
(Rubiyat)

Happy just to get a phone call;
with age your hope keeps standing tall.
Knowing your strength has passed to me;
my love for you; there to recall.

Plans for your eighty-fifth birthday,
made you glad this news came your way.
Feeling proud the power is there
to give you the joy I display.

Plans for your eighty-fifth birthday,
made you glad this news came your way.
Feeling proud the power is there
to give you the joy I display.

Aware one thing would excite you.
Trying hard; this thing I could do.
No gift could tempt you except this.
My heart with thoughts you know are true.

Guessing my precious tiny pup,
only the size of a teacup,
could make you feel so full of glee;
a gift; to bring your spirits up.

Nothing else can be done right now.
Mother's Day gift, you won't allow.
You'll wait for that day in July;
bless the sense I guessed this way how!

~*~

Discovering
(Rhyming Couplets)

Belonging merely to a place traveled;
where darkness to solely me unraveled.

Knowing the secret fold to slip within;
where consign of a mind grasps not the sin.

Beyond the blackness seen by too many;
tranquility's light invites not any.

Discovering beyond obscurity,
a hidden doorway into purity.

Isolated, emerging in my view;
awarding this spirit thoughts to construe.

~*~

Love
(Quinzaine)

**Affection is felt close by.
Does someone love me?
Who is it?**

~*~

Magic Fairies
(Rime Couee)

Once upon a time, way north, in a land,
lived an evil man, who thought to expand.
Pretense on the outside was nice.
He used lies and banishment to command;
was confused when things did not go as planned.
He'd have to learn to pay the price.

**Playful fairies began to feel offended;
retaliation was not intended.
In fairyland all good wins.
Mean man got old as gray beard descended.
Good people left him feeling quite splendid.
Now, living with kindness begins.**

**Fairies know how to make others at ease;
magic is alive and floats in the breeze.
Mean old man did not comprehend.
Fairies try to be polite and appease;
magic fairies also have expertise.
Friendship and love, they do extend.**

~*~

No Title
(Sijo)

Animals reluctantly; ravenous investigate.
Starvation desperately progresses arrogantly.
Provisions, energetically vivaciously, existing.
~*~

Overcome
Naga-Uta

**Tree lost many leaves
Seems like dying piece of earth
Loss of will to live
Soil continues natures force
Land has existence
It will preserve over time
Life on earth will overcome**

~*~

Author's Note:
A Challenge by Mary Ann Duhart.

Dreams Unfolding
(Cyrch a chwta)

Time traveling through the clock;
for fragrant scent people flock.
Where to go past two o'clock?
What treasures lay to unlock?
Gem may be under a rock;
will it be found on a walk?
Dreams unfolding with a chime;
never ending time; tick tock.

~*~

Integrity of Your Way
(Cinq Cinquain)

Begin
love from within;
for it has always been,
the best way for love to step in
and win.

~~*~~

Display
to her, each day,
you really must convey
the integrity of your way,
today.

~~*~~

**Desire
can burn like fire,
when lovers can acquire
caring gentle words to inspire
prior.**

~~*~~

**Tell her
that you concur
her love you do prefer,
because you are a connoisseur
demure.**

~~*~~

**With me,
you must agree;
for this I guarantee,
in such love with you she will be,
you see.**

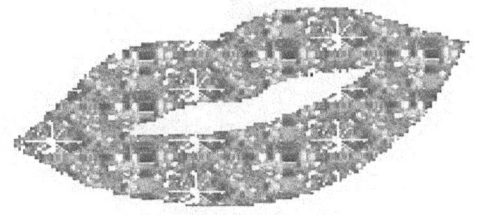

~*~

My Essence Sings
(The Tree)

You
and me
together.
Do try to see
us two forever.
For certain always be,
in all good and bad weather;
in hopes on this we can agree.
y
o
u
and me.

∽∽*∽∽

Let
me grow;
spread my wings.
Don't halt my growth.
There are many things,
which can inspire us both.
Lust for life; my essence sings.
Make this pleasure of life our oath.
L
e
t
me grow!

∽*∽

Teardrop
(Kyrielle Sonnet)

Heard there can be magic in life,
when a woman becomes a wife.
There has to be a reason why;
wondering why love makes me cry.

Answers do not come readily;
tears tend to appear steadily.
Could ask but there is no reply;
wondering why love makes me cry.

Emotions build with good and bad;
coming when sensations are glad.
Sensing a teardrop in my eye;
wondering why love makes me cry.

Heard there can be magic in life,
wondering why love makes me cry.

~*~

Gazing at Stars
(Rondeau)

Gazing at stars; lazing on moon,
soaking in memories of June,
of a night she went to explore.
Stepped into a dazzling door;
shimmering light brilliantly strewn.

**To the voice with the silver spoon;
of this longing never immune.
Man in the moon she did adore;
gazing at stars.**

**Angel engrossed as she does swoon;
she who hears him quietly croon.
Excitement she could not ignore;
never been in reach of before.
Vocalizing to his own tune,
gazing at stars.**

~*~

AUTUMN HAS BEGUN

(Haiku Suite)

**sun descends in sky
haze of dimness starts to form
sun dissolves in earth**

~~***~~

**trees casting shadows
night encompasses forest
cool breeze approaches**

~~***~~

**nighttime winds are crisp
sweet silence overcomes land
autumn has begun**

~~***~~

leaves thinning from trees
multicolored blanket forms
God's painting begun

~~***~~

ginger and amber
shelters earth from early frost
God's airbrush design

~*~

Blonde of All Trades
(Rhyming Couplets)

Personality is getting split;
throwing my head in a great big fit.

At night, instead of going to bed;
in front of my computer, I'm led.

When I finally do fall asleep,
it's with bunnies and eggs in a heap.

Turning into a computer whiz,
this blonde is losing lots of her fizz.

Part of the time, I do web design.
Sonny learned about take-out to dine!

Videos are a big part of me;
silence in the house is the big key.

Phones, doorbells, barking and Sonny's moves;
he's still waiting till my mood improves!

Now, have become a computer tech;
know how to do it, so what the heck?

At times it would be nice to just write
if wireless printer would work right!

I have become a 'Blonde of All Trades;'
got to utilize before it fades.

~*~

Don't See What to Wear
(THE AMPHIGORY)

Don't see what to wear.
Will it match my hair?
My doggie is brown;
should I wear a crown?
The bed is not made;
will the color fade?

Don't see what to wear.
I really don't care!
Husband hurt his back;
papers did attack!
Will you make dinner;
need to get thinner!

Don't see what to wear.
I've got so much flare!
Now, where is that pill?
Just not feeling ill!
Will I have to share?
I love my meat rare!

Don't see what to wear.
The music will blare!
Do you wash your clothes?
I can't see my nose!
Computer is on.
Did you see I'm gone?

~*~

Author's Note:
A Challenge by Joree Williams.

She Dances on Air
(Cyhdedd Hir)

Silently appears;
she has no more tears.
Gone are all her fears;
floats with the breeze.
Devoid of earth's woes;
from her head to toes.
Happily she glows;
moving with ease.

~~*~~

There is no despair;
not even a care.
She dances on air
with expertise.
Her caution did cease;
basking in release.
Smiling and in peace,
in all she sees.

~*~

Magical Dust
(Lilibonelle)

Discover allure of the rose;
let magical dust blow through air.
Unearth heart; ascertain true key;
even picturesque wings can tear.

Let magical dust blow through air;
lure of temptation is greedy.
Insatiable lust dies in time.
Adhere not to become seedy.

Unearth heart; ascertain true key;
use it wisely and hold it dear.
Unlock; check for changes within;
inadvertent deeds can bring fear.

Even picturesque wings can tear;
cleverly use key to a heart.
Angel with a torn wing will fly.
With strength from within, she'll depart.

~*~

World Peace
(Villanelle)

World peace is the decree.
Life is now very sweet.
All people do agree.

No need to ever flee;
now, everyone can meet.
World peace is the decree.

United by land and sea;
such a lovely treat.
All people do agree.

There is a guarantee;
let us sing on the street.
World peace is the decree.

Oh what a jubilee;
decision is concrete.
All people do agree.

Mankind all free;
life feeling complete.
World peace is the decree.
All people do agree!

~*~

World in Her Hand
(Mid-Swap)

She can have the world in her hand
with courage to take a firm stand.
Past reveals future; listen well.
What will be we cannot foretell.

Endowment bestowed upon you;
many tasks lie within your queue.
Let love of others guide your path,
lest world receive a heavy wrath.

All things can be at her command.
She can have the world in her hand.

All eyes will scrutinize choices;
beware of thunderous voices.
Examine where you are going;
be not deceived in all knowing.

Encompassing the gift of youth;
knowledge has power of found truth.
Time is her ally that she may expand.
All things can be at her command.

~*~

Within Salvation
(Daveda's Dix-Par-Deux)

**Realization gives light to queries;
secures eyes shut to unwanted theories.**

**Vanishing from harsh reverberation;
seeking harmony within salvation.**

Banish

**Hope dying with each episode endured;
cruel agony stands firmly assured.**

**Denunciation only solution;
creating ultimate retribution.**

Discard

~*~

Mere Mortals
(Rhyming Couplets)

131

Beyond interim, mere mortals amble,
cause not the motivation to shamble.

Imminent transformation lingers close;
uninitiated die in morose.

Sensitivity channels those favored;
opportunity allows gifts savored.

Hush, for not all can encompass rewards;
which illumination will guide towards.

~*~

Glossary

Abecedarian
In an Abcderian, each line begins with a letter of the alphabet, A-Z; the use of rhyme is up to the poet; there are always 26 lines in this classic type of abcderain. There is a triple abcderian where there are three words per line with the same letter beginning each word; then there is the mesostich abcderian where the middle words spell out the alphabet; then the double abcderian is where the first and last words in a line correspond to the alphabet; there is also the zyxudarioan which is a reverse abcderian. One famous example of the Abecedarian can be found in classical Hebrew poetry: Psalm 118 in the Douay-Rheims numbering of the Bible (119 in the King James version) is an abecedarian acrostic, with each stanza headed by one of the letters of the Hebrew alphabet (Aleph, Beth, Gimel, etc.).

Acrostic
In acrostic poetry, the first word or the first letter in each line will spell out a secondary message if read in sequence. Variations of this theme include having the last word or letter of the line spell out the message. Acrostic poetry can be rhymed or not, strictly metered or Free Verse. Acrostics appear in literature as early as the third chapter of the Book of Lamentations.

Ameri-ku
A poetry style by Carl W. Harris.
6/6/5/5/4/4

Must be about love.

THE AMPHIGORY
is a nonsensical poem that makes no sense but appears to do so. It is kind of like a nursery rhyme. This form can take after any form in poetry; everything is up to the poet; rhyme, accent, syllables, stanzas, lines are all optional. I put the rules in the a-z page the only rule is that the poem must make no sense or be nonsense.

Ballade
This French format contains three stanzas of seven or eight lines, plus a four-line envoi that repeats the last four rhymes of the previous stanza. Syllable count is the same in each line. It uses no more than three rhymes with an identical refrain after each. The rhyme scheme is a-b-a-b-b-c-b-C; a-b-a-b-b-c-b-C; a-b-a-b-b-c-b-C; b-c-b-C.

Cinq Cinquain
Cinq-Cinquain means "five groupings of five." Each cinquain (stanza, for lack of a better translation) has five lines, each line carefully structured in terms of syllable count. Two, four, six, eight, and two syllables respectively equals twenty-two syllables per stanza. Five cinquains equal one Cinq Cinquain.
Cinquain; Properly, a cinquain describes a person, place or thing. Of the two major types of cinquain, the first is defined under "Cinq Cinquain." The second comes in two versions, governed by thematic style. There is no rhyme scheme, and the thematic structures are as follows. Theme

#1 Line 1: one word; Line 2: two words, describing the first line; Line 3: three words relevant to first line, showing action; Line 4: four words showing feeling; Line 5: one word referring to the first line; Theme #2 Line 1: noun; Line 2: two adjectives, modifiers for line one; Line 3: three word verb clause (or phrase); Line 4: a complete sentence, relevant to theme; Line 5: synonym for the opening noun. Dry.

Clerihew
Humorous format contained in a single quatrain and composed of two rhyming couplets. The rhyme scheme is a-a-b-b with lines of uneven length. Clerihews are usually written as pseudo-biographical pieces about a famous personage. The name of the subject ends the first, or occasionally the second line and the humor is light and whimsical instead of satirical. Edmund Clerihew Bentley (1875-1956) created the format to avoid boredom in school.

Cyhydedd Hir
Line 1 - 5 syllables - rhyme a
Line 2 - 5 syllables - rhyme a
Line 3 - 5 syllables - rhyme a
Line 4 - 4 syllables - rhyme x
Line 5 - 5 syllables - rhyme b
Line 6 - 5 syllables - rhyme b
Line 7 - 5 syllables - rhyme b
Line 8 - 4 syllables - rhyme x

Cyrch a Chwta
An octave of seven-syllable lines rhymed aaaaaaba with cross-rhyme of b in the third, fourth, or fifth syllable of line eight.
xxxxxxa
xxxxxxa
xxxxxxa
xxxxxxa
xxxxxxa
xxxxxxa
xxxxxxb
xxbxxxa or xxxbxxa or xxxxbxa

Cywydd Devair Fyrion
Another of the welsh forms. This one has only four syllables per line. Rhyming couplets. aa bb cc dd etc

Daveda's Angel
was created 07/18/09 (Hybrid Concrete)
Syllables: 1, 3, 1, 10, 8, 7, 6, 5, 2, 2, 4, 5, 6, 7, 8, 9, 10
Rhyme Scheme: a, b, c, c, d, e, d, e, f, g, g, h, i, h, i, f, f
Poem should take on the shape of an angel.

Daveda's Dix-Par-Deux
This is a new style of poetry invented by Daveda Gruber on 03/04/08. The style consists of 2 rhyming couplets of 10 syllables making up each line then a line of 2 syllables (the 2 syllable lines must sum up the 2 couplets they follow) then 2 more 10 syllable couplets and another line of 2 syllables. You can do as many as you wish!

Daveda's Quatre-Rime-Par-Huit
This form was invented on 11/08/08 by Daveda Gruber. Syllables: 7, 5, 3, 1, 7, 5, 3, 1. In a stanza lines 1, 2, 5, and 6 must have the same rhyme. Then over again as many times as you wish. Any theme can be used.

Free Style
Rhyming poetry without a set meter, rhymes always end lines although rhythm and word-flow decide where the rhymes belong. Technically, Free Style can be considered a spin off from Free Verse.

Haiku
Is Japanese form that relies on brevity and simplicity to convey its message... usually three lines of 5/7/5 syllables, and frequently includes natural images or themes ...there is so much beauty in the seasons as they change

Joree's 2 Line Finish
this is a new form; first couplet of each stanza has 6 syllables; 2nd couplet of each stanza has 7 syllables; the last line (the 5th line) of each stanza is the finish to the line before and is 3 syllables; as many stanzas as one wants; each stanza 5 lines.

Katauta
The Katauta verse form was actually used in the Man'yoshu (an early anthology of Japanese poetry). The verse consists of three lines with five/seven/seven sound units.

When this form is doubled, it is called the sedoka. Since the Man'yoshu dealt with a wide variety of subjects, no particular subject or even field is considered out-of-bounds.

Kyrielle Sonnet
A contempary form of the Sonnet, created by forming a union between the Sonnet and the Kyrielle. Eight syllables per line; three quatrains and a couplet.
AabB
ccbB
ddbB
AB

Lanturne
Five lines
Line 1 - 1 syllable
Line 2 - 2 syllables
Line 3 - 3 syllables
Line 4 - 4 syllables
Line 5 - 1 syllable

Lilibonelle
Four stanzas, four lines each. abcb rhyme scheme Stanza 1: Line 1 Line 2 Line 3 Line 4
Stanza 2: Line 1 (line 2 from first stanza) Line 2 Line 3 Line 4
Stanza 3 Line 1 (line 3 from first stanza) Line 2 Line 3 Line 4
Stanza 4 Line 1 (line 4 from first stanza) Line 2 Line 3 Line 4

Limerick

The limerick is a humorous poem of five lines with a rhyme scheme of a a b b a. Lines 1, 2, and 5 have nine syllables apiece, while lines 3 and 4 only have six syllables.
Or:
Write five lines in a humorous way, with a rhyme scheme a a b b a.
While lines one, two and five have nine bees in the hive, with just six, three and four do their say. Note: the faux-limerick has the same basic structure as does the limerick, and usually serves the same function. It may vary in line length, or in purpose. Faux-limericks with serious intent can be found.

Mid-Swap

Created by England's Jenny Buzzard, this form requires adherance to a strict structure. It contains four quatrains with a center couplet, at a syllable count of eight per line. The rhyme scheme is: A1abb ccdd A2A1 eeff ggaA2 Or, to put that in an example:
Start out with a line in rhyme "A," XXXXXXXa XXXXXXXb XXXXXXXb XXXXXXXc
XXXXXXXc XXXXXXXd XXXXXXXd Do once more a line in rhyme "A."
Start out with a line in rhyme "A." XXXXXXXe XXXXXXXe XXXXXXXf XXXXXXXf
XXXXXXXg XXXXXXXg XXXXXXXa Do once more a line in rhyme "A."

Naga Uta

Begin your Naga Uta by counting out five syllables for your first line and seven syllables for your second line, and repeat that pattern throughout the length of your poem. It should look like this: 5/7/5/7/5/7.

Think of ways to use words that make you feel what they say. Naga Uta is also a form of music where drum beats play an important role. As you write your poem listen to the beats of the syllables that you use to write it.

Finish your Naga Uta with two lines of seven syllables each. You poem should look like this: 5/7/5/7/5/7/5/7/7 or however long you wish to make it, as long as the last two lines have the same syllable count.

Nonet

A nonet has nine lines. The first line has nine syllables, the second line eight syllables, the third line seven syllables, etc... until line nine that finishes with one syllable. It can be on any subject and rhyming is optional. Line 1 - 9 syllables   Line 2 - 8 syllables   Line 3 - 7 syllables

Ottava Rima

Format:
Line 1 - rhyme a, Line 2 - rhyme b, Line 3 - rhyme a, Line 4 - rhyme b,
Line 5 - rhyme a, Line 6 - rhyme b, Line 7 - rhyme c, Line 8 - rhyme c.
Ten syllables per line.

Pantoum
Line 1 - Rhyme A
Line 2 - Rhyme B
Line 3 - Rhyme A
Line 4 - Rhyme B
Line 5 - Repeat line 2 (rhyme B)
Line 6 - Rhyme C
Line 7 - Repeat line 4 (rhyme B)
Line 8 - Rhyme C
Continue the cycle carrying the even lines to the odd of the next stanza with a minimum of four stanzas.
EXCEPT FOR the last stanza which is built as follows:
Line 2 of previous stanza
Line 3 of FIRST stanza
Line 4 of previous stanza
Line 1 of FIRST stanza

Quatrain
Four line stanzas of any kind, rhymed, metered, or otherwise. Like the couplet, there are many variations of the quatrain.

Quatrain (mono-rhymed stanzas)
Same as Quatrain but stanzas are mono-rhymed each having the same rhyme throughout the stanza.

Renga
A renga is a series of linked poems of alternating 5-7-5 and 7-7 syllable stanzas. Traditionally there is no theme as each stanza must relate to the previous stanza and the

one below it, yet no three consecutive stanzas are to make sense. The relationship between each stanza and those before and after it is often obscure but is never readily apparent. Renga are written collaboratively with at least two poets who take turns writing each successive stanza. It is worth noting that most oriental languages are unaccented languages so meter is not used.

Rime Couee
(French) I found this version of the Rime Couee in Joree's new book.
Any number of 6 lines stanzas with the syllable count up to the poet; the only stipulation is that every 3rd line must be shorter than the other lines and have the same syllable count with each other; the rhyme scheme is: aabaab; ccdccd; etc.
I used 10 syllables for the long lines and 8 for the shorter ones.

Rondeau
A Rondeau is a French form, 15 lines long, consisting of three stanzas: a quintet, a quatrain, and a sestet with a rhyme scheme as follows: aabba aabR aabbaR. Lines 9 and 15 are short - a refrain (R) consisting of a phrase taken from line one - normally the first few words (four syllables). The other lines are longer, eight syllables.

Rhyming Couplets
Rhyming Couplets are a pair of lines, even in syllable count, which share the same end rhyme.

Rubiyat
This Arabic format has a quatrain wherein the first, second, and fourth lines rhyme. The rhyme scheme is; a-a-b-a. A single stanza can be a poem in itself or multiple stanzas may be joined to create a larger piece. Eight syllables per line.

Septolet
poem consisting of 7 lines containing 14 words with a break in between the two parts. Both parts deal with the same thought and create a picture.

Sonnet (Shakespearean)
Please be advised this form has more form than we have shown here. This is probably the most well known and recognized format in the present day. Though made famous by Shakespeare, the format is much older and there are actually three different sonnet formats; Shakespearean, Spenserian, and Petrarchan (Italian). Each has an unique rhyme scheme but all have fourteen lines. The sonnet may be broken into three quatrains with alternating rhyme and a heroic couplet ending it. Note that when written there are no spaces between stanzas. The petrarchan format has several different possible endings known as tercets (three line stanza). end tercet variants dcd/ddc/edc ; here is petrarchan rhyme scheme abba/abba/cdc/cdc

Sijo
Like haiku the sijo is nature oriented. There are three lines, each with its own syllable count. Each line has a specific

focus; the first line introduces a situation or problem, the second line includes a development, the third line resolves tensions created in the first line or resolves the problem in the first line. Again we must note that Oriental languages tend to be unstressed. Each piece must be self-explanatory, requiring no title
Syllable count: Line one: 3, 4, 3, 4
Line two: 3, 4, 3, 4
Line three: 3, 5, 4, 3

Tanka
5,7,5,7,7 syllables ... the best tanka harmonizes the writer's emotional life with the elements of the outer world used to portray it.

THE AMPHIGORY
is a nonsensical poem that makes no sense but appears to do so. It is kind of like a nursery rhyme. This form can take after any form in poetry; everything is up to the poet; rhyme, accent, syllables, stanzas, lines are all optional. I put the rules in the a-z page the only rule is that the poem must make no sense or be nonsense.

The Tree
Form by Dorian Peterson Potter
8 lines 1/2/3/4/5/6/7/8 syllables..line 9 and 10 are the same words as line 1 and 2..line nine horizontal..line 10 vertical.. any subject..rhyme optional...no verse limit...

Shadow Sonnet
Pick any rhyme scheme from any sonnet; I used the Shakespearean sonnet scheme of abab; cdcd; efef; gg; the sonnet has 3 stanzas of four lines each and a couplet of two lines at the last; the other stipulation is that the first and last words need be the same word or be words that sound exactly alike such as sea and see; oh you may choose either 9 or 10 syllables per line.

THAN-BAUK
A Than-Bauk, conventionally a witty saying or epigram, is a three line "climbing rhyme" poem of Burmese origin. Each line has four syllables. The rhyme is on the fourth syllable of the first line, the third syllable of the second line, and the second syllable of the third line.

Villanelle
Traditional Villanelle: lines are grouped into five tercets and a concluding quatrain ...total 19 lines
Lines may be of any length.
Villanelle has two rhymes ...rhyme scheme is aba, with the same end-rhyme for every first and last line of each tercet and the final two lines of the quatrain.
Two of the lines are repeated:
pattern of line-repetition is as follows:
A1 b A2
a b A1
a b A2
a b A1
a b A2
a b A1 A2

In the above,
The lines of the first tercet are represented by "A1 b A2", because the first and third lines rhyme and will be repeated later in the poem.
The first line of each subsequent stanzas is shown as "a" because it rhymes with those two lines.
Meanwhile the second line ("b") is not repeated but the second line of each subsequent stanzas rhymes with that line.

Wordsmith
Write a poem using a word as in an acrostic going down the left hand side of the page but use the first letter to begin all three words in the line.

More Books by this Author

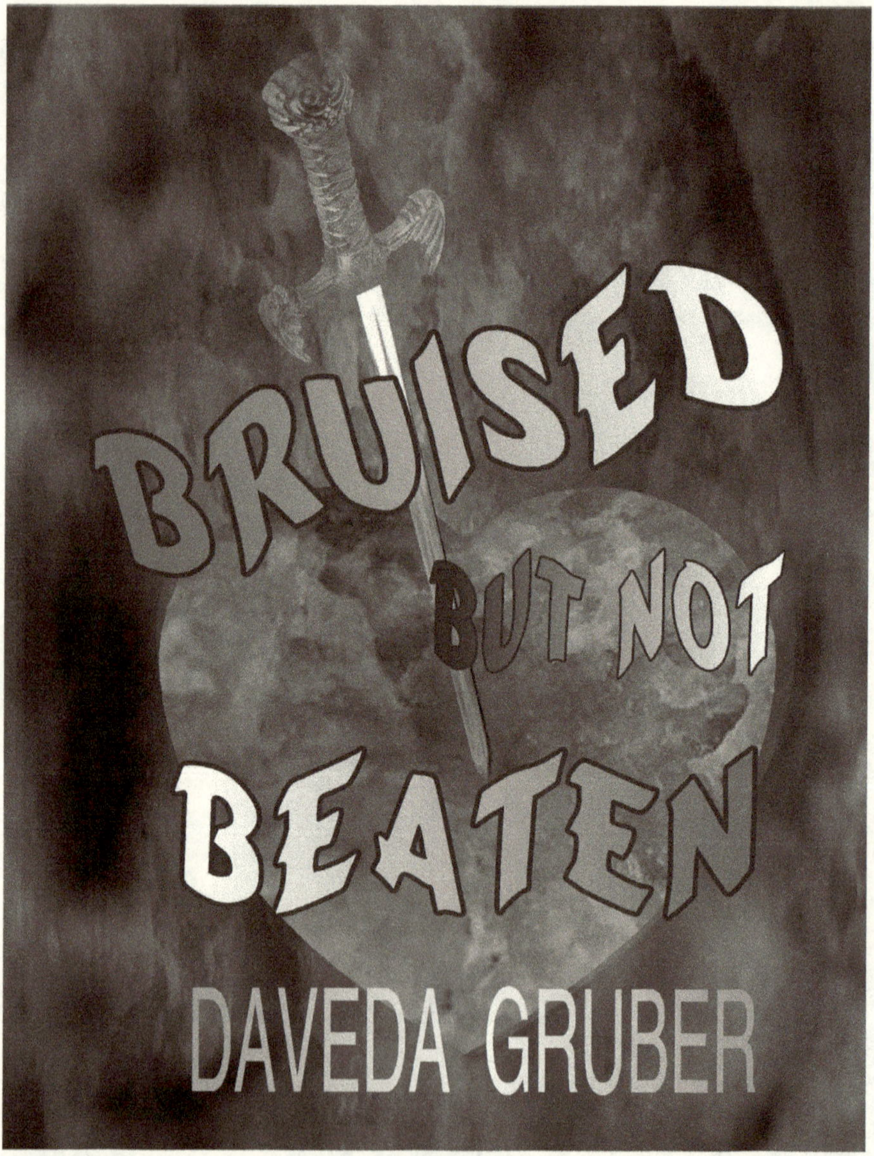
BRUISED
BUT NOT
BEATEN
DAVEDA GRUBER

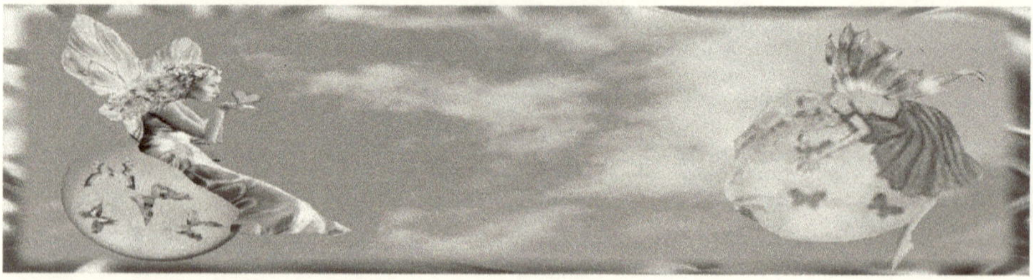

DEATH OF A DAUGHTER

Daveda Gruber

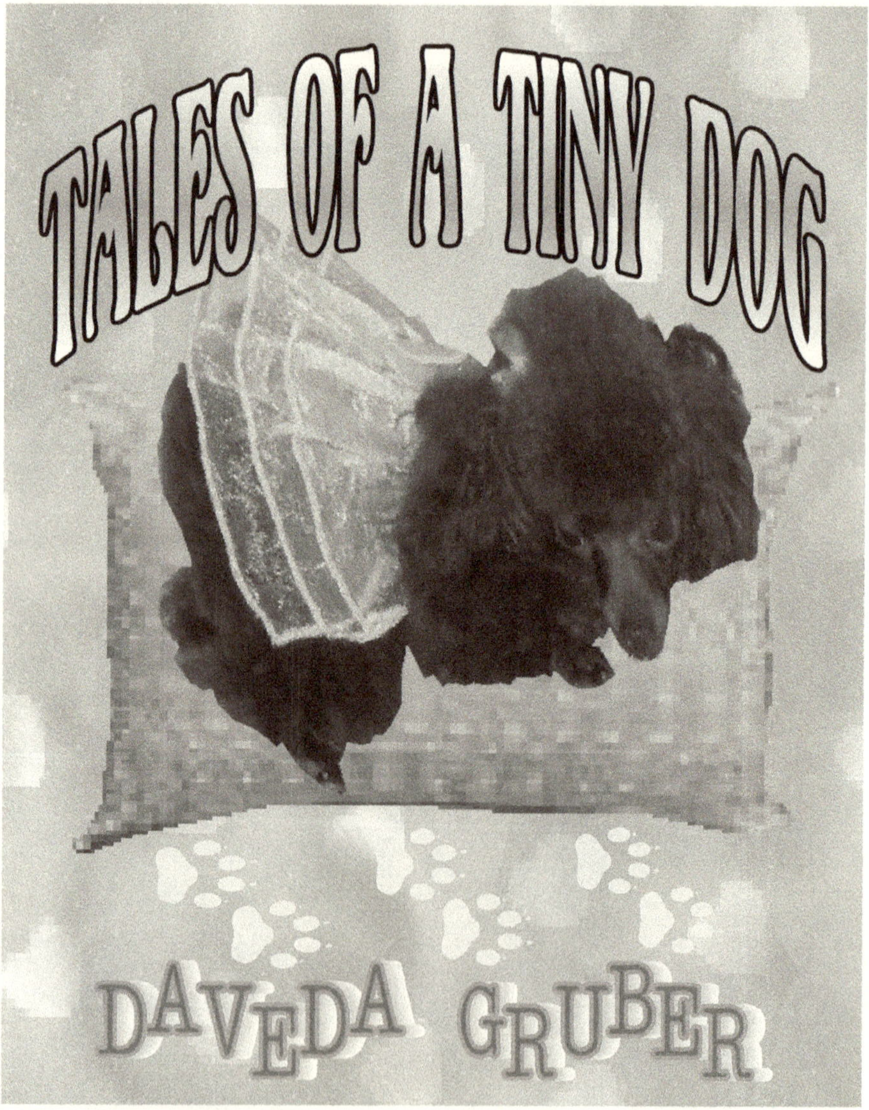
TALES OF A TINY DOG
DAVEDA GRUBER

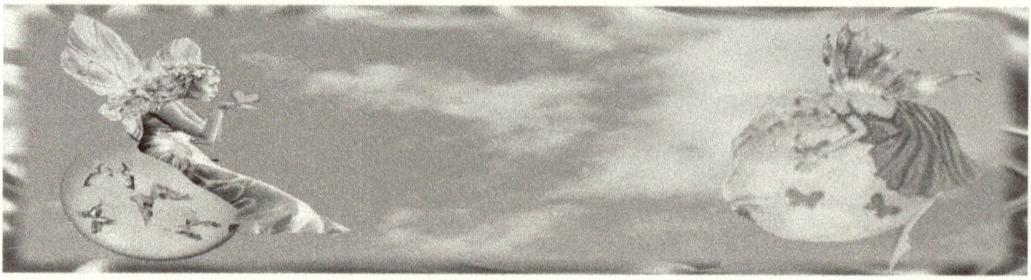

Red Barn and other Short Stories

DAVEDA GRUBER

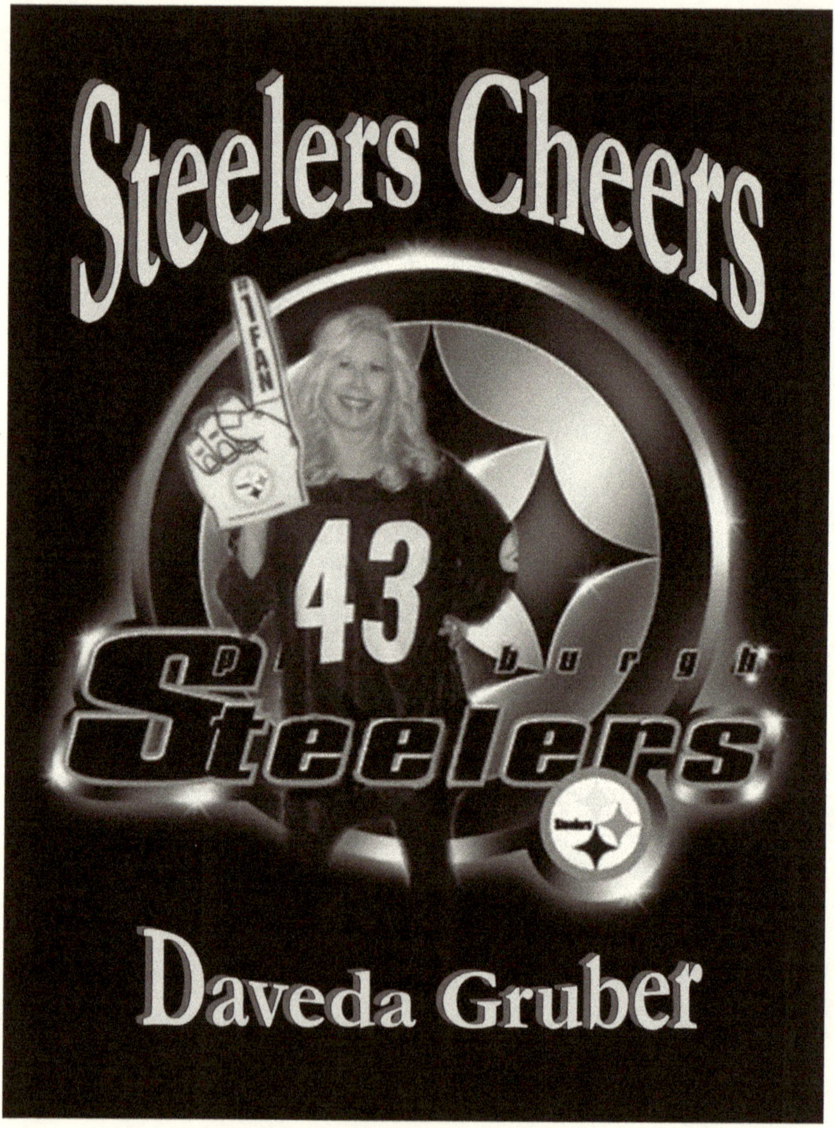
Steelers Cheers
#1 FAN
43
Steelers
Daveda Gruber

http://davedagruber.com

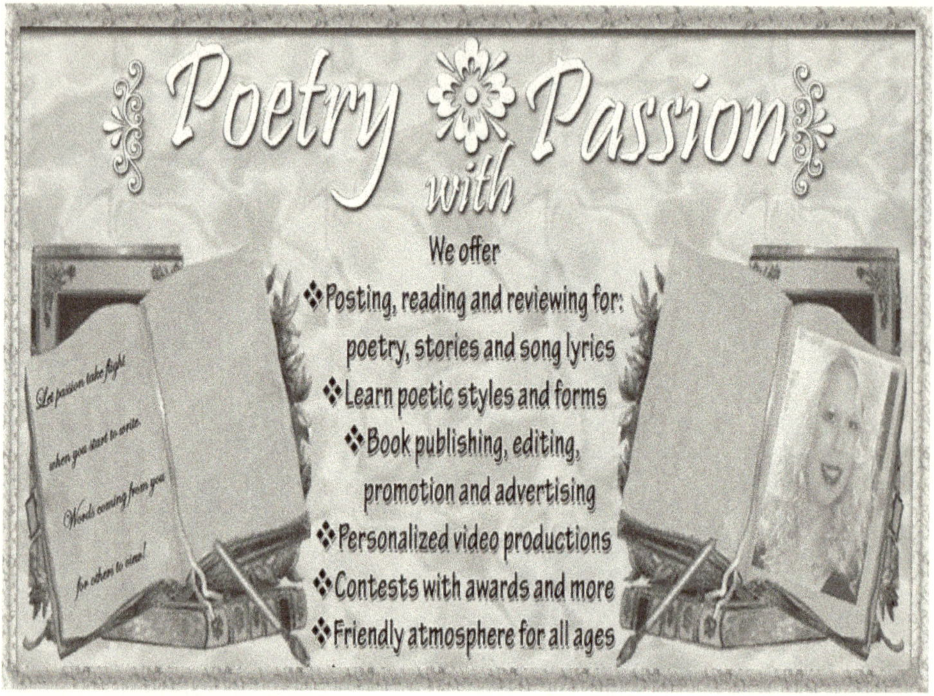

http://poetrywithpassion.com

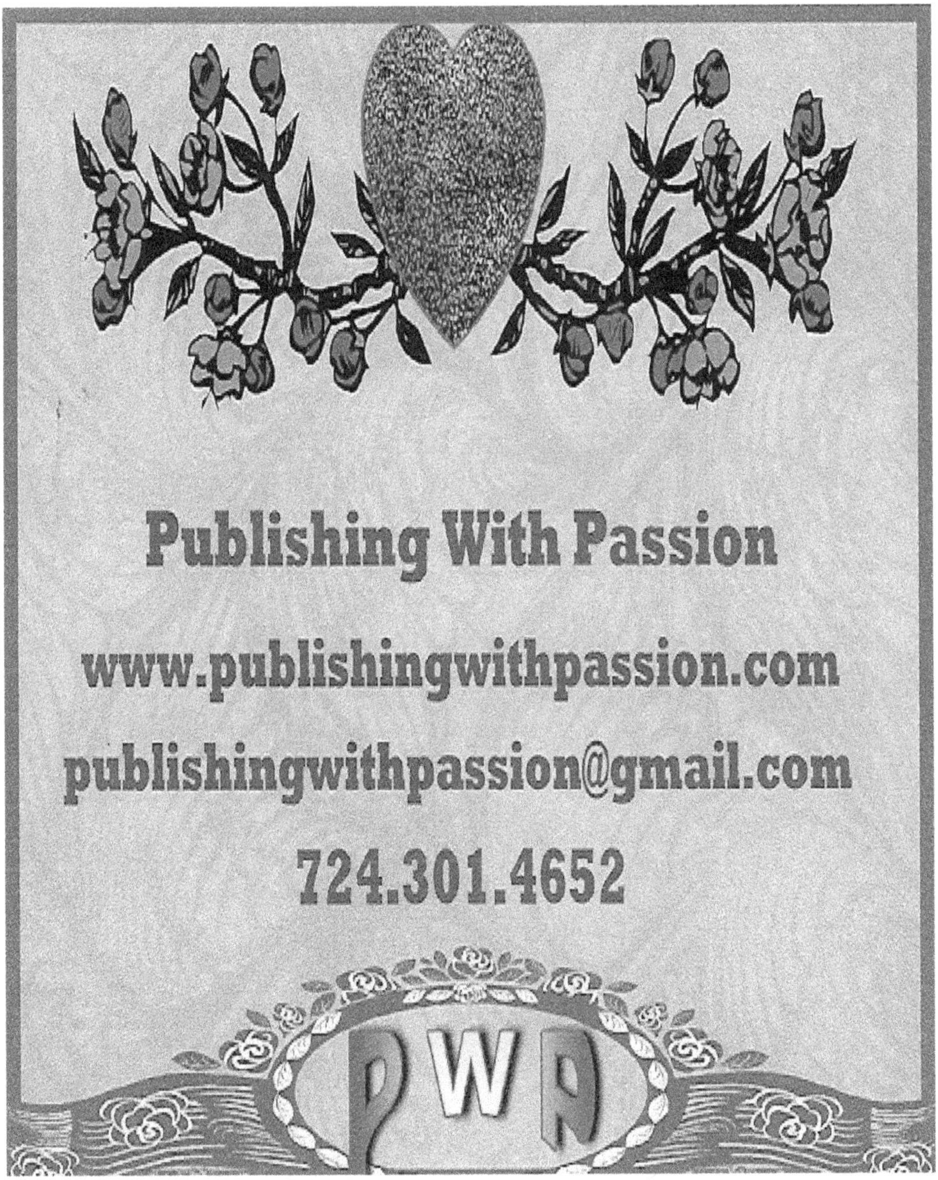
Publishing With Passion
www.publishingwithpassion.com
publishingwithpassion@gmail.com
724.301.4652
PWP

www.ingramcontent.com/pod-product-compliance
Lightning Source LLC
Chambersburg PA
CBHW032119090426
42743CB00007B/405